CHRISTIANITY, FAITH AND IDEOLOGIES

Christianity, Faith and Ideologies

A call to counterculture

Hugo Herrera

Table of Contents

Dedication

«To all those who defend the truth.»

Acknowledgments

To God, for the opportunity to once again use the gifts and talents given to take His message to the world.

To my parents, for teaching me with their example, the important value of family and to each one of my siblings.

To Alejandra Toledo, for her unconditional support in each project.

To Jacob Amado, a great friend and companion in the militia and with whom I can freely talk about such relevant issues for the building up of the body of Christ.

To Marcela Amado, thank you for your support for this work and for your professionalism in the photographs.

To José and Emma Recinos, for their unconditional support for the preparation and completion of this book.

To Gonzalo Chamorro, for your academic contribution to each project.

To Tony Rojas, for leaving your talent and professionalism in each work we do, as well as in each project we carry out.

To Arnulfo Villagrán, for believing and joining each project carried out.

And to the entire team at Editorial CVV for making it possible for this book to see the light.

Foreword

I remember with great pleasure the moments in which together, under the smoke of the barbecue, we shared not only food, but also hours of debate on relevant issues and, above all, those of great influence on culture, trying to reveal the true motivations and objectives of trends accepted as good truths in favor of a better life, but which hide sinister intentions behind that mask of progress.

In this proposal, Hugo leads us to focus our attention on the true causes of the social decline of this time and reveal the truths hidden by these anti-Christian currents that threaten the family.

Throughout my growth as a Christian, I have always been curious about issues of relevance and difficulty that put our truth in tension. For many, these controversial issues are banalities of this world that they prefer to ignore since they are complicated, but in this book Hugo demonstrates the urgency that these ideals are destroying the body of Christ and the responsibility we have before it.

With a simple eloquence, he reveals the problem for us, takes us into the shadows of ideologies where the most concealed and sinister truths are hidden, bringing an open mind to the knowledge of the true intentions, giving us clarity and leaving a concern for change. He gives us tools to defend our faith and to articulate rational arguments that are not against our faith and solidifies our theological positions as true believers.

Hugo explains in a simple way the concepts and foundations of the greatest cultural crisis in the history of mankind. This book is the beginning, not the solution, so that the reader begins to think about the motives and behaviors, not only personal, but those who surround him and those who influence him, be they the society, friendships, social networks or the government.

The moment of transformation that we are experiencing is palpable and it seems that we are only being overwhelmed by this trend of ideologies that pretend to bring answers to an ill society and that the only thing they are doing is trying to kill the patient since everything is based on what Enrique Rojas says in his book El Hombre Light (Light Man) in a nihilistic tetralogy: Hedonism-consumerism-permissiveness-relativity, that is, pleasure is the absolute value. It is this society in which we live that is blinded by these nihilistic values that do not allow them to look at the source of truth and absolute satisfaction that is Christ. The results of this social construction are the destruction of the family as the nucleus of society and, finally, the disconnection of personal relationships and the lack of purpose that leads to depression, stress or anxiety.

Also, Hugo has been a promoter of the fundamentals of the true follower of Christ and has guided us in previous books through the correct motivations that should govern our lives, such as faith and biblical values. Defender of the family as the true foundation of a strong society, he reveals reality and instructs us by delving into the relevant issues that are against us and discovers a reality to which most are asleep, anesthetized or in an ecstasy of digital consumption which does not allow one to think for oneself, but rather to follow the group in ecstasy walking towards the precipice of error.

At the end of this reading, you will be able to come to the conclusion that we are being attacked as a society by an invisible enemy whose objective is to destroy the family and its values and transform the culture by inventing new "values", habits and behaviors based on feelings of the moment and not in the absolute truth. The social order is destroyed and ceases to be governed by the principles of the nature of creation, adopting ideals founded on pure individual pleasure.

This explosion of ideals contrary to God seems to be a total war against Him and His children, confirming the aggravation of the case and the reality in which we are living, which are the final days of this era and the prompt appearance of a massive universal adoption system which will dictate what you can do and what you can't do and even beyond, what you can think and what you can't think, what is right and what is wrong regardless of what you believe or profess. Yes, that's how it is, dear reader, the prelude to the antichrist system.

Rev. Jacob Amado, MSL
Executive Pastor, La Iglesia En El Camino
(Church On The Way)
Los Angeles, California.

Introduction

We live in the 21st century where the progress of changes is accelerated. The economic, political and moral crisis are the ideal excuse for a sociocultural change. This allows for social transformations and other mechanisms such as inclusion to position themselves and take advantage in order to present solutions that guide us to peace, human dignity and gender equality in order to prevent violence and discrimination. Although it seems that their intentions are good, they are nothing more than indoctrination in order to position an agenda through social engineering to have control of the masses, an issue that we have to seriously analyze.

Postmodernity through moral relativism opened a broad scenario that served as a platform for today›s society. For this reason the old values began to be rejected and the moral and spiritual decline is so evident just by watching the news of the day. The values that gave life to the West have been collapsing, especially because of what the «fathers of suspicion of the 19th century» planted in us. Today, the world adapts to the system that is established and positioned daily, and despite the great growth of Christianity worldwide, Christians show little interest in a real Christ, and this is reflected in the behavior of society and, mainly, in families.

This in its nuclear concept, is in crisis and is being attacked like never before in history. God›s design in the family is being devalued and falsely destroyed by totalitarian or collectivist ideologies represented in «gender ideology» and the destruction of the image of God in the human being. Its objective is to convince and guide the individual to a new lifestyle.

Contempt for the Holy Scriptures produces rejection of the model created by God and has caused the collapse of the birth rate, paternity, responsible motherhood and the belief in marriage with the aim of destroying the family institution. For these reasons it is so urgent to promote a «theology of the family» to create a reformation in biblical family life to remind humanity of God›s design.

Times have changed, children no longer practice the same customs and beliefs as their parents; the heritage of Christianity is diluting to smaller groups. It is enough to see the reflection of the United States, a nation that was born with Judeo-Christian principles but which have been forgotten. In my travels through its different States, I have observed churches in large buildings but with an enormous absence of congregants; it is evident that previous generations not only did not know how to connect and transmit the legacy of Christianity, but also the addition of this current of ideologies and new customs encourages the questioning and redefinition of values in the new generations that causes them to be inclined to live as they see fit, belittling the scale of Christian values.

We can then say that the crisis of faith that is experienced today is due to the forgetfulness of the Holy Scriptures in the family nucleus, because the family is the foundation of society and when it loses its values, it loses its vital engine, its essence. The way to destroy it is to disintegrate it, for this reason we should not be surprised that we live in a world that is constantly attracted and seduced by evil, which accepts and promotes it, turning people into insensitive beings.

This is also due to the entertainment industry that grows with great success through plots of terror, murders, tragedies and, generally, everything that destroys nature, human and animal life. That is why it should not surprise us to see the misfortunes that the news reflects daily.

Enough already! The world is setting the guidelines for us on how our moral behavior and way of thinking should be governed, when it should be the other way around, that is, Christianity should set the moral guidelines with principles and values that only the Scriptures can provide.

Faced with all these social changes, we must ask ourselves the following question: Could it be that God was wrong and the changes have led Him to modify the plans for humanity? To think of an affirmative answer is crazy... but sadly for many Christians it is so. It urges us to recognize and be honest that as a Church we need to believe in the truth once again, eliminate errors and restore the Christian faith.

The purpose of this book is to create awareness and reflection in today›s society so that we can find a way to equip ourselves to face the challenges posed by the contemporary scenario, because we cannot adapt to what the world does, if we do we are dead;

but if we dare to change, the world will have to adapt to values that only Christianity can be capable of upholding.

Hugo Herrera
Miami, November, 2022

Chapter 1

The Difference Between Ideologies and Ideas

In recent years we have seen the great sociocultural change that has been taking place due to the rethinking of traditional concepts, the questioning and redefinition of values, the mixture of this has allowed them to focus on ideals that turn out to be decisive in culture.

Today so many changes are generated, we see countries that can be destabilized and controlled by those who have the power to punish in case they do not support an established agenda. In such a controlling system, we must ask ourselves: What is it that moves the world? Is the government interested in having ignorant people? Is the education we receive truly good?

Therefore, in this chapter we want to explain the difference between ideologies and ideas to have a better understanding and see in which direction the world is heading and the way in which the new generations are affected by this system that is established every day, due to to the rise of technology, social networks and the effortless way to get information.

1.   Ideologies

Ideology is made up of two words of Greek origin: idea (ιδέα) and science (λόγια) which means "science of ideas".

The concept of ideology was born at the time of the French Enlightenment at the end of the 18th century and the beginning of the 19th century. Destutt de Tracy[1] is credited as the creator of this term, although its meaning was not respected, since his intention was to promote an objective and liberal philosophy. The aim was to return ideas to their place, as products of certain mental and physiological laws. De Tracy's fortunes were short-lived, however, as Napoleón[2] began to renounce revolutionary idealism and gave it a pejorative meaning by calling him and his fellow charlatans:

"You ideologists," he complained, "destroy all illusions, and the era of illusions is, both for individuals and for peoples, the era of happiness."

In the year 1812, on the eve of his defeat in Russia, Napoleon addressed[3] the ideologues and blamed them:

"To the doctrine of the ideologues to this diffuse metaphysics, which in an artificial way tries to find the primary causes and build on these bases the legislation of the peoples, instead of adapting the laws to the knowledge of the human heart and the lessons of

---

1. See Terry Eagleton: "Ideología" (Ideology) (Edit. Paidos, Buenos Aires 1997) P. 96

2. Ibíd. P. 98

3. Ibíd.

history! History we must attribute all the misfortunes that have befallen our beloved France!"

As we can see, ideology appeared not only as a science of ideas, but as a set of abstract ideas, illusory to a certain extent, without effective correspondence with the reality of man and his history, which are nevertheless used as a matrix from the which to force a new way of existing, dubbed in a new legislation established for that purpose.[4]

Years later the ideology would gain more strength thanks to Karl Marx and Friedrich Engels, creators of the famous "German Ideology", which we technically know as the "Marxist Ideology". There are others such as Chinese, religious, American Ideology, to name a few, and one of the most popular in our time is "gender ideology."

It is ironic to remember that ideology began to exist precisely as a science, as a rational inquiry into the laws that govern the formation and development of ideas, however, its use today is nothing more than manipulation and imposition to exercise absolute control.

Ideologies are statist because they seek the support of the State and Government to be able to impose themselves. What used to be an option is now an imposition with legal consequences if what is approved by the government is not accepted, as is the case with gender ideology today. In some laws, those who rise up against these ideological movements can even be charged with hate crimes.

---

4. Agustín Laje: "La Batalla Cultural" (The Cultural Battle) (Edit. Harper Collins México 2022) P. 134

In conclusion, we can say that ideology is a normative set of emotions, ideas, beliefs, and collective customs that are compatible among themselves to determine the individual's social behavior.

We can then say that ideologies are built, not born individually. They tend to be static and whoever suffers from it, thinks that their reality in that set of ideas is valid for any case without depending on any context. An ideology has a representation of an ideal, but at the same time it seeks public policies to impose itself.

We have explained the term ideology, below, let's see, idea.

2.   Ideas

We can define it as an image that exists or is formed in the human mind contemplated in its ability to use its reasoning. In other words, it is the mental representation that arises from the reasoning or imagination of the person who creates it.

The art of thinking is the most sublime manifestation of intelligence. An idea is what moves us to achieve something, for example: "I had the idea of going on vacation" or "I had the idea of buying a new car." Also a "fixed idea" can be the main reason to achieve goals in our lives: "Since I was a child I had the idea of being a professional actor." They are even used in expressions "I must get used to the idea that everything is over"; It is also used to describe a lack of knowledge or ignorance: "I had no idea about the situation", "I had no idea about this topic".

The concept has several ways in which the word is often used. For example, in psychology: "the delusional idea" is characterized as a pathology of several ideas that are not modifiable by the subject and that cannot be carried out.

In short, an idea is a mental representation of anything. Ideas are dynamic, as Hegel pointed out, and they can evolve, change, and are driven by open minds in search of the truth.

Although there is a difference between Platonic philosophy and what we are explaining, I do not want to leave out what is postulated in the famous "Plato's Theory of Ideas"[5] that are classified into two: "sensible" is what is found in objects, everything that can be perceived by the senses, that is, everything physical. And the "intelligible" are the forms and ideas. For Plato, ideas are the model of sensible things, therefore they are nothing more than a copy of the ideas. In other words, everything that starts in the human mind as an image can end up becoming a reality.

God has created us in His image and likeness, therefore, human beings have the ability to think, generate ideas and create (Proverbs 2:6).

In conclusion, the difference between ideologies and ideas is that the former are built and do not arise individually, while ideas are individual and evolve. Once this difference is understood, we can continue to develop how these ideologies dominate much of the world through the manipulation of language in our next chapter.

---

5. For more information see "La teoría de las ideas de Platón" (Plato's Theory of Ideas" (Edit. Universidad de La Plata 2016), they can also be consulted at www.memoria.fahce.unlp.edu.ar

Chapter 2

The Manipulation of Language

Human beings by nature will always follow whoever manages to empathize with their ideals or convinces them otherwise. Let's not forget that history has been told by the victors, the right to write it was one of the privileges granted by victory. As George Orwell points out:

"Who controls the past controls the future, who controls the present controls the past"[1]

This phrase from Orwell is so revealing because of what is happening today; a cultural battle is being waged that leads to education and the media being manipulated and controlled by the interests of those who are behind this totalitarian dominance that wants to be established in the world, and if they manage to win, they will end up writing history.

The objective of this chapter is to explain how through the manipulation of language the individual becomes more permissive, sees everything as something normal and the way in

____

1. Cited by Bernal, Anastasio Ovejero "Fundamentos de psicología jurídica e investigación criminal" (Fundamentals of Legal Psychology and Criminal Investigation) (Edit. Salamanca, Salamanca 2009) P. 82

which it ends up affecting a society. We will divide this chapter into two: absolute mind control and inclusive language.

1.   Absolute Mind Control

The media exerts great control over the masses. When seeing the behavior of today's society, it should not surprise us how easily the individual is manipulated through his emotions due to the bombardment of information that is published and that, thanks to the digital world, is at his fingertips. There is an elaborate system whose purpose is to control the masses that they call "the globalist agenda"[2], established to end nations, their identity and sovereignty, destroying itself the culture in which they are founded. They seize their wealth, obtaining political and economic control that will also lead to the imposition of an anti-family policy that will drastically reduce the world population and provide solutions and defenses to like-minded people.[3]

The plan of the globalist agenda is very ambitious and through the manipulation of language the systems for the domination of the masses are established. It can clearly be controlled due to the extraordinary power wielded with great success by the large transnational communication companies such as Comcast, The Walt Disney Company, AT&T and ViacomCBS[4] that control the information and entertainment that is consumed on the

____

2.   Dr. César Vidal defines it as a supranational agenda in order to have global control. For more information see Cesar Vidal "Un mundo que cambia" (A Changing World) (Ed. Agustin Agency, Nashville 2020) P. 105

3.   Ibíd.

4.   Ibíd.

planet and, of course, the rest of the smaller companies, but with great influence, such as Sony Corporation and Fox Corporation, which join to distribute the information.

Yes, these transnationals exercise extraordinary control over where we should go and what we have to consume. We should ask ourselves, then, what has led societies today to be so easy to manage and that there is little intellectual curiosity.

Antonio Cruz calls it "the death of ideals"[5] which is nothing more than the description of the contemporary individual as one who lacks absolute certainties since nothing surprises him, so he can easily change his mind, as easy as it is to change a shirt, as a result of the computer avalanche with which he faces daily due to the diversity of currents of thought that transforms him into a vagabond of ideas without knowing where he is going.[6]

This is not far from the reality of current social behavior, especially in the new generations because when we lose the ability to rationalize, we are more vulnerable to being dominated and heading towards any current of thought and the globalist agenda is positioned more strongly for the domain and control. It is so significant to see that values are being lost and are undervalued due to the effect that this liquid society7 in which we live has on us, which has resulted in an intellectual decline because it is no longer important to debate ideas, now everything is allowed

---

5. Antonio Cruz, Postmodernidad (Postmodernity) (Edit. Clie Barcelona 2003), P 52.

6. Ibíd.

7. Differences arise when reason is not sufficiently awake or when it falls asleep again. See. Zygmunt Bauman "Modernidad Líquida" (Liquid Modernity) (Edit. Argentine Economy Culture Fund, Argentina 2002) P. 179.

and not the moral bases, principles and absolute truths matter. In other words, moral decline leads to intellectual decline; Scripture is blunt when it speaks about it:

> *"Do not be like the horse or like the mule,*
> *Which have no understanding,*
> *Which must be harnessed with bit and bridle,*
> *Else they will not come near you."*[8]

The verse is forceful and very clear, the difference is that animals were created to proceed by instinct and human beings by intelligent decision. We can say that if societies are easily manipulated, it is because each individual is not using their ability to think and analyze what is happening around them, or they simply remain on the sidelines for various reasons, such as fear, and that automatically makes them socially ignorant.

Christianity must be the benchmark for culture change and counteract the manipulation of social engineering, and not be enslaved by a manipulative system. (Romans 12:2). Scripture is once again clear: *"that you may become blameless and harmless, children of God without fault in the midst of a crooked and perverse generation, among whom you shine as lights in the world"* (*Philippians 2:15*).

Let's not forget that the stars shine brighter when darkness dominates, based on this we are those luminaries in a world of darkness. The globalist agenda tries to control the world, so we should never forget that we are the resistance and those who prevent them from consolidating themselves by the scale of

---

8. Psalms 32:9

values and moral principles that we possess as children of God. We must give an answer so as not to perish in ignorance. Jesus said: "*And you shall know the truth, and the truth shall make you free*"[9] If we stop teaching this, we will be dominated by lies and that will end in us being slaves to the system.

In our next section we will see how they intend to impose a new way of speaking under the pretext that no one should be excluded.

2. Inclusive Language

Inclusive language is in fashion, widely used among youth with the idea of making a better world to avoid discrimination through the modification of words.

In the title of this section we find the union of two concepts, let's define what each one means. First, language: it is the faculty of the human being to express himself and communicate with others through articulated sound or other sign systems.[10] We can also say that it is the means by which human beings can express their ideas, emotions, feelings, etc. Second, inclusive: it includes or has the virtue and ability to include[11]. Now, if we join these two concepts, it means that inclusive language is a means of communication that includes.

Language defines who we are, this means that the words we use are the basis for connecting with others. With them

---

9. John 8:32

10. See. Language www.dle.rae.es (Viewed 11-18-2022)

11. Ibíd.

we express ourselves and understand the world by building a culture. The problem is when there are changes in semantics and linguistics, nobody can think without using words, therefore, if they change the words, they will end up changing the culture.

Inclusive language aims to provide a solution to not discriminate and include everyone, because it determines that the language used in society is a historical cultural component whose principle is the supremacy of men over women. Faced with this, it is intended to provide a solution not only for women but for all those who do not identify as part of a binary gender, that is, those who do not identify as neither man nor woman.

What does inclusive language itself aim at? Simply establish a new form of communication, that at the moment of expressing yourself, does not make anyone invisible. This includes all genders and identities through a modification of the semantic and linguistic use and breaking supposed sexist, patriarchal ideas and discriminatory attitudes in order to establish a value of gender diversity.

Agustín Laje calls it "the cultural battle for language"[12] in which societies have bought the talismanic[13] words that lead us to be prisoners of an ideology. This is nothing more than a dystopia where the terms are inverted as mentioned by George Orwell[14] in his work "1984". With these inversions, we will end

---

12. Agustín Laje "Ideología de Género y Aborto conferencia" (Gender Ideology and Abortion conference) published November 16, 2021 See. https://youtu.be/EU4G5RsE0vs (Viewed November 18, 2022).

13. Its meaning: Object to which a magical power is attributed capable of giving health or luck or of benefiting the person who has it in their possession.

14. See. In George Orwell's magisterial work "1984"

up calling the good bad and the bad good[15], as it also appears in the behavior of the people of God.

Inclusive language, proposes to replace certain words with others. For example, we are in an auditorium and the presenter greets "Hey you guys!" This would automatically be offending because it excludes women and those perceived to be of another gender. If the word "girls" is used, it would be the other way around. The inclusive proposal is to avoid offending and not exclude anyone. They are also used in other types of groupings as in the following table.

Not Inclusive	Inclusive Language
Mankind	People, humanity
Policeman	Police officer
Spokesman	Spokesperson
Salesman	Sales associate
Fireman	Firefighter
Hostess	Host
Waitress	Server

The United Nations Organization (UN) calls it 'gender inclusive language'[16] and mentions in this regard:

"By gender-inclusive language is understood the way to express oneself orally and in writing without discriminating against a particular sex, social gender or gender identity and without perpetuating gender stereotypes. Since language is one of the key

---

15. Isaiah 5:20

16. See. Gender inclusive language www.un.org (visited 11-18-2022).

factors determining cultural and social attitudes, using gender-inclusive language is an extremely important way to promote equality and combat gender bias."

Gender ideology, as we mentioned in the previous chapter, is statist because it takes refuge before the State to legalize and with the support of the government to create a collective indoctrination in this modality of language.

Now, if we want to fight a cultural battle of language, we must do it as citizens and as Christians. The way to avoid not excluding anyone is to change our social behavior by being more friendly, such as: "Good morning! Good afternoon! Thank you! Please!" Sadly, most of the new generations of today no longer greet nor thank.

We must be grateful and respectful, this does not mean that "respect" is synonymous with "approval". We must defend our values with arguments, wisdom and education. Scripture tells us:

"Who is wise and understanding among you? Let him show by good conduct that his works are done in the meekness of wisdom. But if you have bitter envy and self-seeking in your hearts, do not boast and lie against the truth. This wisdom does not descend from above, but is earthly, sensual, demonic. For where envy and self-seeking exist, confusion and every evil thing are there. But the wisdom that is from above is first pure, then peaceable, gentle, willing to yield, full of mercy and good fruits, without partiality and without hypocrisy. Now the fruit of righteousness is sown in peace by those who make peace." *(James 3:13-18)*

The text is clearly understandable for our time. Today we see that there is a fascination for gender diversity and one of the ways to position it is through education and dissemination in the media. Gender ideology does not provide reasonable coexistence, but rather promotes differential rights against all those who oppose these issues. Therefore, in order to create a counterculture in this regard, we must follow the indications of the biblical text, training ourselves to be understood in these times to counteract ignorance and manipulation (1 Chronicles 12:32).

So far we have seen how the manipulation of language modifies and indoctrinates the behavior of a society.

Next, we will see the consequences of what this all leads to.

Chapter 3

The Acceptance of Ideological Change

The apostle Paul explains to us in Romans 5:12 how sin entered the human being and that by nature we inherited[1] evil and we are all sinners. In James 1:14 we see that the evil that dwells in us exposes us to temptation. Epithymia[2] according to the Holy Scriptures is a reality which we will have to deal with every day of our lives. In other words, activating evil is just one step away, therefore, hating it or practicing it will depend on the kind of spiritual life we practice. In the context of our society, it seems that it is easier to end up accepting everything, sometimes it is for fear of losing stability and economic position, or simply for living in a double standard. We are part of a narcissistic society where hedonism is lived in its greatest expression. Selfishness is not strange at all, since the important thing is to seek personal pleasures and achievements as taught by Ayn Rand who proposes

---

1. Humans are heirs by divine decree of innate sin with all its consequences. For more information, see Raúl Zaldívar, "Apocalípticismo" (Apocalypticism), (Edit. Clie. Barcelona. 2012) P.28.

2. Based on James 1:14. This verse is the key to the entire passage, since it affirms without any ambiguity of any nature that the inclinations to do evil come from the concupiscence of the man who in the Greek language would be called Epithymía, which could be translated as desire or passion, but in reality it is a vehement inclination of the soul towards that which is contrary to the will of God. To expand this study further, see Raúl Zaldívar "Doctrina de Santidad" (Holiness Doctrine), (Edit. Clie. Barcelona. 2001) P. 70.

that "selfishness is a virtue".[3] Under this pattern it doesn't matter what happens to others.

Acceptance of ideological change seems to be normal and unfortunately the church also does it, even when this human practice is contrary to the model of life established in the Holy Scriptures, and before that we have to give an immediate response.

For this analysis we will divide the chapter into two: Gender Ideology and Legal Deaths: Abortion and Euthanasia.

1.   Gender Ideology

Gender ideology is one of the main strategies of the globalist agenda. Gender ideology advances with three powerful weapons: LGTB+[4], legal deaths (abortion and euthanasia) and radical feminism.[5]

In the first instance, let's define: What is gender ideology? The core idea of gender ideology[6] is to explain that our sexuality is

---

3.   Ayn Rand develops a collection of essays in which she presents her moral code, such as rational egoism and her opposition to the prevailing morality of altruism, the duty to sacrifice for others. See Ayn Rand "The Virtue of Selfishness", (Ed. Signet USA 1964).

4.   After the sexual revolution and the rise of its diversity, the acronym LGBT arises whose meaning is: L= lesbians, G= gay, B=bisexual, T=transsexual. However, in recent years it has been expanded, so the + sign is used at the end of the acronym (LGBT+). Generally we see that the rainbow flag represents the expression of the collective.

5.   Radical feminism is a current that maintains that the root of social inequality is patriarchy, as the system of oppression of men over women.

6.   Gender ideology views the natural family, as God created it, as a zombie institution that walks mortally wounded, and should no longer even be replaced

not determined by the genitals that are traditionally known as male and female, but has been attributed to the social context. One of the most accurate definitions of gender ideology is what Agustín Laje points out.

"It is a set of anti-scientific ideas that for authoritarian political purposes uproot its nature from human sexuality and explain it exclusively from culture."[7]

In the media, with great aggressiveness, we see daily the aspects that Laje mentions in this description. Gender ideology aims to establish that each one can determine what they want to be according to how they perceive themselves inside. Given this, we cannot leave out the manifesto of contrasexuality that opposes the sexuality of human nature. Beatriz Preciado[8] explains in detail:

"Contrasexuality is not the creation of a new nature, but rather the end of nature as an order that legitimizes the subjection of some bodies to others. Contrasexuality is, first of all, a critical analysis of gender and sex difference, the product of the heterocentric social contract, whose normative performativities

---

by the tribe or community that were aspirations of postmodernity, but should be replaced by the concept of individual, where the value of the commitment is cheapened and diluted in a floating and individual love, without responsibility towards the other, its main asset being the fluidity of momentary feelings. See Juan Varela, Homosexualidad pastoral de la atracción al mismo sexo (Pastoral Homosexuality of Same-sex Attraction) (Edit. Clie, Barcelona 2016)

7. Agustín Laje, La ideología de género aplasta la libertad (Gender Ideology Crushes Freedom). Published March 5, 2019. https://youtu.be/RDeoYGq-2GHM (accessed November 19, 2022).

8. See. El manifiesto contra la sexualidad (The Manifesto Against Sexuality). www.revistadelauniversidad.mx (viewed 11-19-2022).

have been inscribed on bodies as biological truths. Second, contrasexuality aims to replace this social contract that we call nature with a contrasexual contract. Within the framework of this contract, the bodies recognize themselves not as men or women but as speaking bodies and recognize others as speaking bodies."

In other words, it means that at some point in history, we agreed to determine who would be men and who would be women.

This manifesto is nothing more than revealing of what is happening today because the ambition of gender ideology leads us to the end of nature and the sexes as we know them, even when it is absurd because it is anti-scientific.[9]

Science recognizes the binary gender, that is, male and female. We will explain it in a scientific way and for this we will take Dr. Catherine Scheraldi's[10] concept as a basis so that we can understand how sex is determined in each person, according to studies of genetics[11] and embryology.[12]

"In the nucleus of each cell there are genes with different

---

9. These ideologies do not have a sustainable base in science and are opposed to anatomy, biology, embryology, genetics, psychobiology, among others.

10. Catherine Scheraldi de Núñez is the wife of Pastor Miguel Núñez, and is a medical doctor, specializing in endocrinology.

11. Genetics is a branch of biology that studies how characteristics and physical traits are passed from one generation to the next. To understand that inheritance, look at the genes found in the body's cells that have a special code called DNA (deoxyribonucleic acid).

12. Embryology is the subdiscipline of genetics (according to the UNESCO code), it is the branch of biology that is in charge of studying morphogenesis, embryonic and nervous development from gametogenesis to the moment of birth of living beings.

combinations of DNA, the hereditary units that determine not only the physical characteristics of the person, but also the functioning of each organ. The different combinations in the DNA determine the characteristics of human beings: hair color, skin tone or any other characteristic that marks the individuality of each being. In humans, there are 23 pairs of chromosomes (46 total); 22 pairs are known as autosomes and appear the same in males and females. In addition, there is a last pair that we call "sex chromosomes". There is a difference here: females have two X chromosomes (XX) and males have one X and one Y chromosome (XY). Sex is determined by the type of gene that the fetus receives from his or her parents. The son or daughter receives one sex chromosome from each parent. The mother will always donate an X chromosome and the father sometimes donates an X chromosome and sometimes a Y chromosome. Although sex is determined at the time of conception, in the fetal state, the development of both sexes is identical until the sixth week. If the fetus is male, a protein known as the SRY protein will come into play, which is produced from a gene on the Y chromosome. This protein causes the formation of the male organs. If the SRY protein is absent, the female organs will develop. Thus, the genetic makeup (what we call the genotype) is what determines how the individual looks and functions (what we call the phenotype)".[13]

Not in many cases, but in some, there are cases known as intersex that is traditionally known as true hermaphroditism[14],

---

13. See: Catherine Scheraldi and Miguel Núñez, "Revolución sexual" (Sexual Revolution) (Edit. B&H Nashville, 2018) P. 106 and 107.

14. The so-called true hermaphrodites, which Ann Sterling includes within the group of intersexuals and whose frequency is very low, can present ovaries and testicles simultaneously (so-called true hermaphroditism). In other cases, the ovary and the testis develop together in the same organ, forming an ovotestis. It is not uncommon for at least one of the gonads (most often the ovary) to function

that is, they are born with both genitals: male and female, however, the sexual charge will never be (50%-50%) since one will always dominate and that will be the one that identifies to which sex he or she belongs.

We find ourselves in the midst of an unprecedented sexual revolution created in an artificial way. Its ideas are not renewing but destroying the bases that offer stability to society. What response could we give to the statement that there is more than one binary gender? The Sacred text recounts God's design from the beginning.

"So God created man in His own image; in the image of God He created him; male and female He created them." (Genesis 1:27)

Here we clearly see that God's plan was to create a binary gender: male and female. God created each one with characteristics to perform the function He gave them.[15] Therefore, He would give an identity to the human being because being created in His image and likeness offered a unique value, and this would produce a great blessing in the construction of the family.

The concept of marriage is based on the understanding that, by their nature, men and women are capable in different manners and when the conjugal union occurs, they complement each

---

well enough to produce eggs or sperm and functional levels of the so-called sex hormones (androgens or estrogens). Outside of this group, the rest of the intersex are not fertile. See the article published by the Autonomous University of Mexico https://ciencia.unam.mx/leer/963/-sabes-que-es-la-intersexualidad-

15. Catherine Scheraldi and Miguel Núñez, "Revolución sexual" (Sexual Revolution) óp. Cit. P. 14.

other and acquire new capacities, such as procreation.[16] That is why it should not surprise us that the identity of creation is under attack as never before in history. The change in language has generated what we knew as "biological gender" is now called "assigned gender"[17] regardless of how it looks at birth.

As we have seen, biology, embryology and genetics show that there are only two sexes. This notion that gender is independent of biological sex is considered an ideology precisely because it is not based on science. The population is being indoctrinated and although in some cases it goes against their values, it seems that it is easier to accept it than to oppose it.

In education, it is legalized to indoctrinate children, adolescents and university students in gender ideology. Also the different norms approved with the pretext of not discriminating have created programs for gender ideology and have prohibited psychological treatments for those who want to get out of homosexuality, and whoever opposes this may have consequences such as losing their job or going to prison, as in some cases in Spain.[18]

Gender ideology has also infiltrated Christianity, just add the so-called "inclusive" editions of the Bible that have erased the teaching of homosexuality and conform to the translation of

---

16. Ibíd. P. 103.

17. Which means that this was "assigned" at birth by medical personnel, without knowing if it will be the gender with which the boy or girl will identify.

18. César Vidal "Un mundo que cambia" (A Changing World) op. Cit. P. 192.

gender ideology. We also find "queer theology"[19] which holds that God Himself, or at least Jesus, was homosexual.

Faced with this, how should Christianity respond to gender equality? What to do in cases of homosexuality?

For these questions, let's see the recommendation of Juan Varela:

"First, Christianity must be comprehensive, that is, have a sensitive approach that helps us understand these complexes in depth. Second, it must prevent, by situating and explaining each of the genetic and biological aspects of the family and cultural system to find what are the deficiencies and gaps that paved the way for the loss of identity. And third, Christianity must intervene by acting and consolidating to develop the necessary steps to follow for healing and the recovery of the person's identity.[20]

The world continues to move forward, the decision is ours, if we want to belong to the group of those who resist or of those who remain silent due to the cowardice of not wanting to take action on the matter, even when this puts our family at risk. In the Sermon on the Mount, Jesus warns us about this:

"You are the salt of the earth; but if the salt loses its flavor, how

---

19. Queer theology is a theological current that has developed from the philosophical approach of queer theory, built on scholars such as Michel Foucault, Judith Butler, among others. Queer theology is based on the principle that the diversity of genders and sexual orientations has always been present in human history, included in the Bible.

20. Juan Varela, "Homosexualidad" (Homosexuality) op. cit. P 17, 67, 111.

shall it be seasoned? It is then good for nothing but to be thrown out and trampled underfoot by men." (Matthew 5:13)

In ancient times, salt was used to preserve food. This comparison of Jesus is so drastic because it refers to a society in which the truth is diluted because of sin; society tends to rot and become a putrid mass. So the only way this society won't be spoiled is by salt, and Christianity is salt. But if we keep quiet, we will be trampled and shamed.

Later, Jesus continues with another illustration, referring to the fact that we are the light of the world[21] and, therefore, bearers of the truth that must be reflected at all times, bearing the fruit to illuminate and defend the truth in the midst of all these ideologies that stalk us today. Because if we remain silent, we will be approving it, like the famous phrase that Martin Luther has coined: "Not to oppose error is to approve it; and not to defend truth is to suppress it." Therefore, Christianity is the salt and the light, and we must act immediately.

We developed the theme of gender ideology based on the effect it causes on the identity of human nature and how society has ended up accepting it. Now, about the reduction of the world population.

2.   Legal Deaths: Abortion and Euthanasia

One of the great movements of gender ideology is the drastic reduction of the world population through legalizing abortion and euthanasia. Christianity has been the force to defend life

---

21. Matthew 5:14-16

as a gift from God and by offering a compassionate embrace to the weakest; Christianity has socially promoted the behavior of abhorring such atrocities, even penalizing them (Exodus 20:13).

2.1   Abortion

In the 21st century it seems that the vision of abortion has been changing to the point of considering it a lesser evil, the argument used mainly by radical feminist movements or the symbol of the green scarf[22], is that it is a right that women cannot be deprived of. Each woman owns her body and therefore she can do whatever she wants with it. This type of propaganda is seen by society as something normal.

As it is world news, the Supreme Court of the United States annulled the ruling on the case Roe vs. Wade, which means that now the different states of that country can ban abortion. However, abortion identities such as Planned Parenthood come to the defense under the pretext of presenting immediate help and clarifying that it is still legal:

"Some states have already banned abortion and others have created many restrictions. But abortion is still legal in many states, and it is also legal to travel to other states to perform an abortion. Abortion is NOT prohibited nationwide. The laws on this subject are changing rapidly. We want you to know that we are here to help you understand these new laws and how they may affect your options when it comes to getting a safe and legal abortion."[23]

---

22. This is the case of the green scarf, whose intention is to exclaim equal rights before society for a specific purpose. The green scarf symbolizes the right to legalize abortion.

23. See. https://www.plannedparenthood.org/es/temas-de-salud/aborto/

Planned Parenthood points out "we believe your body is yours" and charges that the new state laws banning abortion are confusing, scary and just plain wrong. This organization makes it clear that it will do everything possible to continue to provide a full range of sexual and reproductive health services, including abortion.[24]

Some time ago I went to give a conference at a church on gender ideology. One of the workshops that I gave to a group of young people was about abortion. During the presentation I asked the question: What do you think about legalizing abortion? A 14-year-old girl raised her hand and replied: "If I want, I can have an abortion, in the end, I decide if I want to have the baby or simply not." This girl not only accepted the abortion, but she was also convinced that she could do it if she got pregnant. It was alarming to me that she was the daughter of influential church leaders.

This is nothing more than a reflection of how the new generations accept these measures even when what is happening is a murder. Because according to science, from the moment of conception[25] or fertilization, there is already life, and that makes her a mother. That is, the woman can decide to be the mother of a living child or the mother of a dead child.

---

todavia-es-legal-obtener-un aborto

24. Ibíd.

25. Science has reliably demonstrated that human life begins with fertilization, that is, with the fusion of an egg and a sperm. From that moment on you are in the presence of a new being, which will develop in a coordinated, continuous and gradual manner.

Christianity must question whether moral values are really being planted in the home or whether youth simply see them as part of a family and cultural tradition, opening up the possibility of thinking and acting differently.

Given this, it is worth mentioning that the practice of abortion was common in the ancient world and has existed for millennia.

In the laws of the Ancient East (Babylonian and Assyrian[26]) it was punished when a pregnant woman was mistreated with various penalties, depending on the consequences of the injured. Hammurabi's code[27] punished abortion with an economic sanction according to the social category of the woman. Abortion in the ancients was something beyond the homes and was considered a social issue. For God's people the law was much stricter (Exodus 21:22-25). Illustrious people like Plato and Aristotle did not hesitate to suggest the practice of abortion as a way of limiting the number of children.[28] Primitive Christianity condemned abortion based on its elevated concept of the value of the human person, extended to the fetus.

Tertullian explicitly states that causing an abortion is the same as committing murder, since the fetus is a human being in the making.[29]

Christianity throughout history has been the resistance against this despicable practice.

---

26. Consulted in: "Diccionario Enciclopédico Bíblico Ilustrado" (Illustrated Biblical Encyclopedic Dictionary) Op. Cit. P. 15 y 16

27. See. (Arts. 209-214).

28. See. (Rep. 5.9) (Pol. 7.14.10).

29. See. Apología contra gentiles (Apology Against Gentiles), XI 8).

Currently we hear different discourses on abortion with their end goal to not affect moral ethics under the pretext that women have the right to choose. For example, in cases of rape, unwanted pregnancies, malformations or limiting the number of children so as not to affect the household economy, among others. Gabriel J. Zanetti[30] concludes the following:

"Abortion is murder. Therefore, one cannot speak of the "right to abortion". That is an absolute contradiction in terms. There is no right to do something that goes against a fundamental human right. Nor can it be framed within the "right of the mother to dispose of her own body." The mother may have the right to freedom from coercion over the disposition of her body, but not over the body of another person. Nor can abortion be classified as "private actions" that do not harm third parties, since abortion eliminates the life of a human person. Then, it is light years away from a private action, on the contrary, it falls within one of the most typical crimes against third parties: murder".[31]

Being pro-life and being against abortion for a Western culture should not be strange under the foundations that formed it, however, it is quite the opposite today because by opposing these movements it makes us "religious fanatics" and "stupid".

---

30. He is a professor and has a degree in Philosophy from the Universidad del Norte Santo Tomás de Aquino (UNSTA) and a PhD in Philosophy from the Catholic University of Argentina (UCA). He is a full-time professor at the Universidad Austral in Argentina, a full-time professor at CEMA, Argentina Visiting Professor at the Francisco Marroquín University in Guatemala, and academic director of the Acton Institute. He is a prolific writer (both of books and articles) and an important Latin American thinker. He has reflected on economics, philosophy, ethics, psychology, epistemology, theology, hermeneutics, education, cinema, and many other topics.

31. For more information, see the article on abortion published by the Crux Institute ttps://institutocrux.org/blogs/buen-arbol/etica/2019/08/sobre-el-aborto-segunda-parte/

As if that were not enough, show business has been commissioned to potentiate that ideology. Singer, Miley Cyrus, posted on her social networks a photo in which she is licking a cake with the message "ABORTION IS HEALTHCARE."[32] This initiative was applauded by other artists and not to mention thousands of adolescents who follow her and approve abortion because their favorite artist defends it. In this way, a Netflix series "Sex Education", promotes sex and abortion in adolescents as the solution in case of pregnancy. In this series, those who oppose abortion are seen as fanatics and stupid (referring mainly to Christianity).

The indoctrination is not at all alarming, Hollywood backed by this abortion agenda is pronounced in such a way that it normalizes this atrocity so that it seems something insignificant as if it were an upset stomach that you can get rid of by visiting any abortion clinic.

For Laje, abortion companies "disguise"[33] their intentions behind sexual and reproductive rights and simulate altruistic concerns for women.

It has been 50 years since the publication of the book "The Limits to Growth" and the conclusion of this text is still valid: *"If the present growth trends in world population, industrialization, pollution, food production, and resource depletion continue unchanged, the limits to growth on this planet will be reached*

---

32. See https://www.lavanguardia.com/muy-fan/20190606/462706545782/miley-cyrus-aborto-desnudo-instagram.html

33. https://www.ucc.edu.ar/mediosucc/ve_detras_del_aborto_presion_internacional_agustin_laje_escritor_dio_una_conferencia_en_la_arena_sonora-8056.html/

sometime within the next one hundred years." The solution to this challenge would be nothing more than *"zero growth".* The famous phrase of Lyndon Johnson is also valid: *"Less than five dollars invested in population control is worth a hundred dollars invested in economic growth."*[34] In other words, the collapse of the economy can be controlled through the reduction of the world population, mainly in poor countries, because in a certain way it ends up affecting the richer countries. The globalist agenda in its essential dogmas is found in its manifestation in the Movement for Voluntary Human Extinction.[35]

Grosso modo, the reduction of the world population is more than an ambitious project since it is promoted in the celebrated 2030 agenda with the approach established in its list of objectives, and which each country involved must comply with.[36]

2.2   Euthanasia

Another issue concerning legal deaths is euthanasia. The word "euthanasia" comes from the Greek eu, and thanatos. Which means a death without pain and in peace (good death).

---

34.   Eduardo Galeano "Las venas abiertas de América latina" (The Open Veins of Latin America) (Edit. 21st Century 2004, Mexico) P. 20.

35.   Founded in 1991 by Les U. Knight and located in the United States, this group calls on mankind to refrain from reproducing in order to lead to the gradual extinction of the human species. Les U. Knight had come to the confusion that most of the misfortunes suffered by the planet were due to human beings. That is why he joined Zero Population Growth. Taken from Cesar Vidal "Un mundo que cambia" (A World That Changes), P. 198

36.   For more information, see the article published on the United Nations website. https://www.un.org/sustainabledevelopment/es/poverty/

The discourse in the promotion of euthanasia is based on the dehumanization of a particular group: the terminally and mentally ill, the disabled and the elderly. This is achieved through the manipulation of language; when defending euthanasia, it constantly appeals to a supposed "dignified death" or "life unworthy of being lived." In this way, a new category of human being is created that can be deprived of life if a third party so wishes.[37]

At present, the term euthanasia has gained more interest in different contexts, whose both ethical and legal assessments are different.

Generally, the word "euthanasia" is used when something is done or not done in the final stage of a patient's life. Technically, euthanasia is also understood as the so-called "compassionate homicide", that is, causing the death of another human being out of mercy for his suffering and in this way fulfilling his wishes to die for whatever cause.

The media campaign and the manipulation of feelings goes beyond the vulnerability of those who cannot bear the idea of seeing a loved one suffer, such as legitimizing the extermination of their peers. In other words, the family member has the right to decide when it is time for someone to die.

The budgets for these advertisements to legalize it are extremely amazing, they seek to have the collective approval and other agreements such as the exhibition of films such as "Mar adentro" (The

---

37. Guadalupe Batallán "Dignos hasta el final" (Worthy To The End) Ebooks P. 522

Sea Inside)[38] which has won awards in which feelings come to the fore with the speech of "a life unworthy of being lived" and the best is death. How is euthanasia performed and what are the ways?

We will explain in the following table the different forms.

Name	Description
Active Euthanasia	When death is caused by an action, such as the administration of lethal doses of medication.
Passive Euthanasia	When death is a consequence of the omission or interruption of treatments whose objective is to maintain minimal life support, such as hydration and food.
Voluntary Euthanasia	When the patient with mental clarity requests that he be killed to free himself from his physical or moral suffering, which he considers unbearable.
Involuntary Euthanasia	It is considered for those patients who for whatever reason cannot give their consent.

Death is inevitable, it awaits all of us. Sometimes God allows a person to suffer long before death comes.

Based on Romans 8:28, God's purposes are accomplished through a person's suffering. However, no one enjoys suffering, but it does not justify, under any circumstance, someone being ready to die.

On the other hand, the elderly also represent a political social bur-

---

38. Based on true events, it tells the story of Ramón Sampedro, a quadriplegic. The film shows his life 28 years after suffering an accident and his struggle to get help to die.

den because it affects the economy due to pensions, food vouchers and all the medical services that are granted to them. For a society that feels bothered with the elderly, the legalization of euthanasia is nothing more than its solution. Annihilating the elderly opens the door to enjoying holidays without inconvenience, because it allows them to make the family schedule more fun and even speeds up the deadlines for collecting the inheritance.

The drastic reduction of the world's population through abortion and euthanasia are the successful advancement of gender ideology regardless of the fact that all this cost is for the death of innocents. Christianity must respond wisely because according to Scripture, it is only God who gives and takes life (Ecclesiastes 7:15-17, Job 12:10).

We do not want to conclude this chapter without first remembering what was previously mentioned in the message of Jesus. We are the salt, we need to get out there, be seen and preserve the truth. The salt inside the salt shaker is useless if it is not used. Therefore, a Church that only relates to itself will not be able to evangelize or present a defense against these ideologies.

Next, we will see how these events end up affecting the institution created by God: the family.

Chapter 4

The Ideological Phenomenon in the New Family Configurations

We have reached one of the most challenging issues due to the aggressiveness of the constant attack of the society in which we live, because if we are not firm in our convictions, we run the risk of being dragged and diluted in the current of the system due to this ideological phenomenon, which is being implemented in the new family configurations.

Gender ideology exercises control to indoctrinate new forms of human behavior and establish it as part of life that will end up affecting the institution created by God, that is the family. Faced with this, we must begin by defining the true concept of the nuclear family and then situate marriage and family within the theological framework that corresponds to it.

For this study, we have considered dividing it as follows: Marriage and The Nuclear Family.

1. Marriage

The intention of this section is to analyze and reflect on the term "marriage" and how it has been manipulated in our time for the interests of those who it is convenient for. Let's first see what the Real Academia Española (Royal Spanish Academy) (RAE)[1] tells us and how it defines it: "Marriage: The union of a man and a woman, arranged through certain rites or legal formalities, to establish and maintain a community of life and interests." It is important to point out that in this same dictionary it also specifies that marriage, for certain laws, is celebrated in people of the same sex, which we will be analyzing later.

The word marriage[2] comes from the Latin 'matrimonium', which derives from 'mater', which means 'mother' and 'munium', which means 'function, legal quality of', that is, the 'legally recognized function/office of mother'. In other words, we say that it is the union of a man and a woman that denotes the right[3] that a woman acquires to be able to be a mother within the law. Grosso modo, marriage is the beginning of the family and therefore the fundamental basis of a society. It is so important that we understand the meaning and nature of marriage as we live in a Western culture that presents us with a radical redefinition of its concept.

For this reason we want to make it clear enough that marriage is the union of two people to naturally form a family. Juan Varela

---

1. See: https://dle.rae.es/matrimonio

2. For more information see "Diccionario Enciclopédico Bíblico Ilustrado" (Illustrated Biblical Encyclopedic Dictionary) (Edit. CLIE Barcelona 2016) P. 1029.

3. Underlying this word is the Roman conception that the possibility that nature gives a woman to be a mother was subordinated to the requirement of a husband to whom she would be subject when leaving her father's guardianship, and that their children would thus have a legitimate parent to whom they would be subject until their full legal capacity.

says the following concerning the matter:

"Marriage and family constitute the basic cell of society and the first relational framework of every human being. Its importance is absolute, because in it people acquire the educational keys with which they will have to develop in society. All the concepts and guidelines for a human being to develop emotionally balanced, both in his inner world and in his social network of relationships are learned in the context of the family, to the point that we can affirm that family, as a natural extension of marriage, the destiny of the person."[4]

It is clear that before this definition we cannot leave out the account of creation according to Genesis 1 and 2 because it shows us a deep theological reality: the marriage or union between a man and a woman belongs to the natural order for humanity. The binary gender means that the woman is not only the complement for the man (comparable helper) but also the sexual difference makes the union of her gametes[5] produce a new life in the human species. However, gender ideology through the approval of new laws has implemented the legal union of people of the same sex, which is known as "equal marriage." As we have studied previously, we can affirm that it does not exist, due to the conditions of its bond, because if the meaning is derived from 'mater' where the womb that will give birth to a

---

4. For more information see Juan Varela and M. Mar Molina "Tu matrimonio si importa" (Your Marriage Does Matter) (Edit. Clie Barcelona 2012) P. 24

5. A gamete is a sexual cell, in the case of men it is the spermatozoon and in the case of women it is the ovum. Both male and female gametes have to fuse in the process known as fertilization to give rise to an embryo and later to a pregnancy. Gametes are haploid cells, that is, they have 23 chromosomes, half of those of any other cell. This serves so that when the ovule with the spermatozoon fuses, the chromosome endowment of the human species can be re-established: 46 chromosomes. In other words, it can only occur in the union of a binary gender.

new life is generated, it cannot occur when uniting people of the same sex, so what these movements want is to be able to legalize it in order to demand from the State what nature itself cannot give them.[6] This leads us to give adoption rights, equality and all the benefits that are legally obtained in heterosexual marriage. Same-sex marriage was unthinkable decades ago in Western culture, but today it is protected by law and celebrated.

If we put on theological lenses, God has revealed to us the nature of marriage and its obligations. Since God unites man with woman He explains the basic elements of marriage. That is why the man leaves his father and mother and joins his wife, and the two merge into one being.[7] Everything else the Bible teaches about marriage stems from these foundational passages. God, as Creator and Lord, is sovereign over humanity, and that includes our relationships. We can conclude that marriage is a lifelong covenant of partnership between a man and a woman that is established before God and the community.[8]

We conclude that marriage is the most sublime metaphor of God's relationship with humanity, because it is not based on a loving fantasy or lived solely sexually. From the creation account we see that every day that God created something, immediately afterward, He recognized that it was good. Therefore, marriage is healthy only when it is based on the permanence of the sacred

---

6. For more information, the analysis is recommended in the section on El Matrimonio Homosexual (Homosexual Marriage) Nicolás Márquez and Agustín Laje "El libro negro de la nueva izquierda" (The Black Book of the New Left) (Edit. Union Group 2016) P. 202

7. Genesis 2:24

8. To delve deeper into this topic, Jim Newheiser "Matrimonio, Divorcio, y Nuevo Matrimonio" (Marriage, Divorce and Remarriage) (Edit. Poiema Colombia 2019) P. 14 is recommended.

bond in the commitment and fidelity of the individuals and in this way, the marriage bond constantly moves towards the restoration of sanctity.

We have studied the concept of marriage, to continue: the concept of family in its natural condition.

2.   The Nuclear Family

The changes in the last decade compared to previous years have been rapid in the new family configurations. The secular and Christian family[9] has been changing certain things from the traditional to the modern and the postmodern. Today's youth experience these changes as something normal, but surely the previous generations can suffer the blow that this has produced when they see the disfigurement of the traditional concept of the family, because these new conformations are leading us to new themes and even to changes in the use of language as we studied it in chapter 2.

Juan Varela[10] makes an analysis of the socioeconomic and cultural changes from the Jewish tradition through the time of the Industrial Revolution and reaching liquid modernity that caused man to lose his identity by leaving the family:

---

9.   From Latin famulus (servant, slave). In ancient times, the family comprised all blood-related members, implying an entire household and including servants who lived under the same roof.

10.   Juan Varela, a Spanish national, is the founder and national director of the Instituto de Formación Familiar (Family Training Institute) (INFFA) and president of the Centro de Orientación y Meditación Familiar (Family Guidance and Meditation Center) (COMEFA). In addition, he is an international writer and speaker.

"The traditional family within the Jewish culture was the mother who educated her children until they were 6 or 7 years old, then the father took the reins; in this way they not only learned a trade but could also carry out the family business, say a blacksmith, silversmith, carpenter, shoemaker, etc., (we even see Jesus learning the carpenter's trade).[11] For generations this was how families lived. From a psychological level, the families were stable and despite the poverty, there was no identity crisis. The youth grew up with a family model where the responsibilities and roles of each member were clear, therefore, there was a solid family structure that remained for generations giving meaning to the continuity of families. With the advent of the Industrial Revolution of the 18th century, the familiar pattern of artisan manufacturing changed to specialized factories and mass production. The era of large factories begins and the need for more workers gives rise to being absent from their homes. The greater the production, the greater the demand, and that caused the man to be absent from home for longer, taking him away from his paternal role, because man began to be more absent than present. Years later, the man began to occupy and dominate the outside world as a producer and provider, while the woman limited her action to the inner world of her family as a reproducer and caretaker of the home.

Two hundred years later, the following words would begin to sound: identity crisis, family breakdown, stress, etc. The Industrial Revolution brought physical distancing due to absence from home, but the world and civil wars brought emotional distancing due to the lack of internal expressiveness, since millions of the men who went to the great battles had to disconnect their feelings and close their emotional plane, as a psychological defense mechanism to

---

11. See Matthew 13:55 and Mark 6:3

endure the horrors of war and the impact of having to kill other human beings."[12]

As we can see, the absence of the man in the home was the collapse of his identity and this also allowed new family configurations to take place over time. Postmodernity had an impact on the family and caused all this accelerated change in the new family integrations. Today it no longer matters what the traditional family was like, since all its values are branded as outdated and meaningless for today's society; now each individual is the one who determines what he wants to build as a family according to the interpretation he gives it. Let's take a look at some of the new family configurations[13]:

Types of Families	Description
Without children	This type of family is formed by a couple without descendants. More and more couples consciously decide not to have children for multiple, personal reasons. In other cases, the infertility of one or both cannot be medically resolved, which is why they do not have children.

---

12.   Juan Varela, "Homosexualidad" (Homosexuality) op. cit. P. 48.

13.   For more information see https://observatoriofiex.es/diversidad-familiar-los-diferentes-tipos-de-familia/

Biparental	It is the most classic, also known as nuclear or traditional. It is made up of a father, a mother and the biological child(ren). The majority of the population, when thinking of a family, imagines a two-parent family with children. Although the term is being expanded more and more, culturally we can still say that it is the most popular type of family.
Homoparental	They are those that are formed by a homosexual couple (two men or two women) with one or more children. Although it is not a new family, its presence in society has increased significantly in recent years.
Reconstituted or Composed	This kind of family is probably the most frequent nowadays due to the growing tendency towards separation and divorce.
Monoparental	They are made up of a single adult with children. Generally, the so-called "single-parent" families are more frequent, in which the adult present is the mother.
Host/Foster	They are in charge of offering minors in need the best possible environment until they are definitively adopted or until their biological family can take care of them.

Adoptive	They consist of a couple (or a single adult) with one or more adopted children. Despite not having blood ties, they are also families that can play a parental role just as valid as biological families.
Extended	It is made up of several members of the same family who live under the same roof. In this way, parents, children and grandparents, or parents, children and uncles, etc., can live together.

We could continue with the list, however, our intention is that we have a clearer idea of how the type of families and their new configurations are being applied. This is not only due to man's loss of identity when he is absent from home, but also to other phenomena such as language change, legal matters, migration, globalization, technology, science, wars, infidelities, poverty, illnesses, deceit, abuse and violations. This has been the ideological phenomenon that has led us to these new family compositions.

God created the family with a divine plan that is fundamental to the blessing of humanity. As Christians we should not take the biblical teachings out of the family for any reason, because they are the vital engine for us to remain firm in all areas of our lives. Since ancient times, God warns not to turn away from Him (Deut. 29:18). Christian families are the model, so they should be:

- Organized (1 Tim. 3:4 & 5).
- Teaching the Scriptures at home (Deut. 4:9 & 10).

- Live in patience and forgiveness (Gen. 50:17 & 21, Mat. 18:21 & 22).

The nuclear family is the source that transmits culture, and when this institution ceases to function properly, the result is the deterioration of culture. Biblical formation taught in homes will give us the discernment to drive out deceivers and liars (Psalms 101:7). For this reason, it is important not to undermine the concept that pre-exists any deliberate order whose goal is to make the spontaneous concept of nuclear family succumb. The world needs families that follow the teachings of Jesus to have the correct model before society, above all, to bear witness to the rise of technology which we will develop in our next chapter.

Chapter 5

The Ideological Phenomenon in the Technological Revolution

The phenomenon that has arisen from the technological revolution has made life easier for us, since we can immediately connect with the world. Communication is much easier and more effective, but it seems that our lives are governed by an intrinsically digital dependency for interpersonal relationships, entertainment, education, work, meetings, digital purchases, among other things. This rise of technology has introduced us to a lifestyle in which we pay more attention to what is happening on the screen than to the real world.

For this study, we have considered dividing it as follows: Persuasive Technology and Surveillance and Digital Addiction.

1.   Persuasive technology and surveillance

Persuasive technology[1] is nothing more than the new regime of the digital economy. In Silicon Valley there is a group of professionals who are dedicated to creating applications (Apps) and all kinds of strategies to turn the consumer into a digital

---

1. It has been widely defined as technology that has been designed to change the attitude or behavior of its users through persuasion and social influence.

dependent. The most important thing for them is to keep the public's attention.

All apps compete with each other, that is why we see that there are so many methods to get our attention through the notifications that they send us through alerts, vibrations, sounds, messages, etc. At the core of this reactor is the economy of attention. The new digital capitalism is a product and a producer, the tools are the algorithms for this general acceleration and thus have better control over its consumers by keeping the public's attention.

A study carried out by the Journal of Social and Clinical Psychology shows that 30 seconds is the maximum exposure time to social networks and internet screens. It has been considered that there is a risk to mental health beyond.[2] My daily practice can be described as a dependence on the signals that crowd the screen of my phone. But I'm not the only one. We live in a world of strobing addicts.[3]

Globalization has also accelerated behavior to convert the world's population into digital consumers. Buying products from China, Japan, Germany, the US or any other part of the world is now so easy that we only need internet access. Even for food there is no need to make a call, much less leave the house, we can order everything from our mobile phone through an App. Everything is aimed at making the individual only depend on the digital world.

---

2.   Bruno Patino "La civilización de la memoria de pez" (The Fish Memory Civilization) (Edit. Alinza, Madrid 2020). Ebooks P. 7.

3.   Ibíd.

Years ago it annoyed me when I received calls, emails and correspondence from companies that offered me their products. At first I was wondering: How did they get my information? But above all: How did they find out that I was looking for this product? The answer is very simple; I myself have provided information through social networks through the user profile, which is available to everyone, so it's easy to know my likes, desires, aspirations, relationships and more. In this world of computing, it should not surprise us that this information can circulate. The digital economy is based on the recording and processing of massive data.

Through the algorithms they can know what our interests are, musical tastes, foods, etc. And based on this exposure that we make in our searches through Google or social networks, they can determine how to filter and sell the products more easily.

It is easy to realize this, for example, if we search Google for information about a specific sport, then, when we open YouTube, we will have videos related to the subject. The same happens if we buy shoes, clothes or any appliance; we must know that the bombardment of offers will come on all social networks such as Instagram, among others. Let's not forget that the success of the digital economy is thanks to the vigilance of the algorithms that obeys the possibility of these predictions and manipulations.[4]

It is also important to point out that ideology is introduced into the digital world in order to direct us towards the personal

---

4. To delve deeper into digital manipulation, it is recommended to read the analysis of Agustín Laje in the contribution of "Economía digital: el imperio del dato y la vigilancia" (Digital Economy: The Empire of Data and Surveillance) of the book "La batalla cultural" (The Cultural Battle).

interests of those who are behind it to control all our actions. They do this in a spectacular and individual way through psychology where they take advantage of the vulnerability of our emotions.

After the blow that the world received with the coronavirus, the way we relate to each other and introduce ourselves to a digital dependency, accelerated. In the midst of the pandemic, the world did not stop, because thanks to technology, interpersonal, work, educational, personal development, family and friends relationships continued, church meetings continued, and the list could go on. This dizzying system came to replace the way of socializing and set new parameters for world communication.

In our personal meetings it seems that we are no longer present because we are more aware of what is happening on our phone than what is happening around us. This phenomenon arose with the initial expectation that everything had to be free. A group of companies had to find a way to make money without charging users. The first thing they did was advertise and start charging advertisers, then they began with the collection of personal data to ultra-segment the message that they give each of us, and finally, each company needed us to spend more time on their platforms.[5] And in this way, have our full attention.

The enormous volume of personal information exposed in the digital media by our online activity is what they use to manipulate us through our needs and vulnerabilities of the mind detected by behavioral economics, psychology and neuroscience.

---

5. Santiago Bilinkis, "Como nos manipula las redes sociales" (How Social Networks Manipulate Us), published on November 27, 2019; https://youtu.be/8nKCA9h-7BA (August 25, 2022).

In other words, they control us and, although our information is supposed to be confidential, it does not mean that it is foreign to the world of big data information.

The more time spent on digital platforms, the better for them regardless of the valuable time that is lost to be with family and friends, but above all the damage caused by not sleeping due to sleeplessness because of the addiction in browsing the digital platforms, which we will be talking about in our next section.

2.   Digital Addiction

Although it is true, social networks have benefited us because they are to be visible to all; depending on our objective, we can position ourselves quickly. We have entered the era of immediate crowd relations due to free accessibility. We publish everything we want or what we do, and we can even present ourselves with an image that is far from real. This is a situation that is nothing more than the result of digital identity for the search for the largest number of followers and "likes", which is the currency with which social acceptance is traded today.[6] Santiago Bilinkis points out that the digital world "is the narcissistic swamp and from which curiously we do not want to leave".[7]

I am not saying that it is wrong to use social networks, but it is when the reason that stimulates us to use them becomes an addiction.

Some time ago I realized that I was unnecessarily staying up late because I was watching series on the popular platforms of

____

6. Ibíd.

7. Ibíd.

the moment. We have been provided with the number of offers to choose from, and furthermore decide whether to watch just one episode or the entire season. Our time is the most valuable thing and they are stealing it from us. Some companies like Netflix say that "sleep is their biggest enemy."[8]

On a certain occasion, in the middle of a tour, I finished the scheduled activities for the day and went to the hotel to rest. But that particular night, with the lights off, I couldn't get to sleep. What I did immediately was check my cell phone; according to me, it was going to be for just a few seconds. I left it on the nightstand, but I replayed the scene five more times. That night I realized that I had a problem with a cell phone addiction, because I wasn't checking anything related to work, I was just browsing social media. The result of that came the next day, because I woke up with dark circles under my eyes and tired, when it should have been the opposite. We are the society of addicts to the stroboscopic connection, therefore, it is worth analyzing the pathologies that these are causing. Bruno Patino analyzes the following:

"We have lost the nights. The phone screen now lights up the dim light. Its luminosity is reduced to the lowest level, but it does not stop being active. It disturbs the sleep of its owner who knows nothing about the work of ganglion cells on the melanopsin in his retina. He doesn't even know of its existence. They are the cells that send the order to wake up to the suprachiasmatic nuclei in the hypothalamus of your brain, as they confuse the blue light of the

---

8. "Sleep is our greatest enemy." This is how Reed Hastings, the CEO of Netflix, summarized it when asked about the streaming platforms that come out to fight him. "When you watch a series on Netflix and get hooked, you stay up late. Really, in the end, we're competing with sleep," Hastings said. Seen in the article published by the newspaper La Nación see www.lanacion.com.ar

LEDs with the white light of day. The sleeper's internal clock goes off, his sleep is restless. An irrepressible desire invades his stillness, the same desire that marks the rhythm of his days, his life, work, vacations, friendships, loves, thoughts and prayers."[9]

Digital addiction is nothing more than the great success of the attention market that has managed to reduce us to the memory of the goldfish in a round fish tank. This fish has the characteristic of having 8 seconds of memory and every time it turns around, it finds itself in a new world. Patino describes it like this:

"Instead, we are like fish, locked in the aquarium of the screens subjected to the rhythm of notifications and messages. Our minds go round and round, from tweets to Youtube videos, from snaps, emails, PUSH LIVE, from apps to newsfeeds, from provocative messages written by a robot to images filtered by an algorithm, from obviously false data to buzz out of place. Like fish, we believe that we are going to discover a universe at every moment, without realizing the infernal repetition in which the digital screens enclose us, to which we deliver the most precious treasure: our time."[10]

Because if we don't take it seriously it will become addictive and we could have other negative consequences.

The Near Future Laboratory is a work group in which medical professionals and others detected four pathologies: anxiety syndrome, profile schizophrenia, athazagoraphobia, and attenuation.

---

9. Bruno Patino "La civilización de la memoria de pez" (The Fish Memory Civilization) Op. Cit. P. 9.

10. Ibíd.

In the following table we see these mental pathologies described by the Near Future Laboratory[11]:

Name	Description
Anxiety Syndrome	It is manifested by the permanent need to disseminate the different moments of existence, however futile they may be, in all networks.
Profile Schizophrenia	It attacks those who, playing with the possibility of having several different identities on social networks and dating portals, end up not knowing how to differentiate the chosen identities from their own. Trapped in their different masks, they no longer know which one to turn to when it comes to facing real life.
Athazagoraphobia	Fear of being forgotten by their peers, unfolds in new variants linked to social networks that, by constantly presenting the quantified results of each of the actions undertaken in their space, feed the melancholy of those who feel abandoned or subjected to the indifference on the part of their digital contacts.
Attenuation	It alludes to the desperate searches that try to locate an individual on social networks to unhealthy limits.

---

11. Ibíd. P.11.

Perhaps for a sector this does not sound alarming, but I believe that it is necessary to evaluate it. Anxiety syndrome is the most common of these. An Instagram story, a Facebook photo, a tweet, the anguish that accompanies it stems from the panic of not finding the right moment or photo to post for fear that it won't elicit enough approving reactions despite filters and other editing tools that allow you to magnify your content.[12] These pathologies should not surprise us and see them as foreign to us, because in one way or another we all run into that river. How many times are we more aware of what happens in virtual life than in real life? The attention market has made us addicted through an ideology of being present at all times to have greater social acceptance, to achieve success in the different activities that we carry out. Electronic stimuli dominate us, we are in "alert mode" all the time, pending the number of comments, likes, views, and messages we receive based on everything we publish. Our social life revolves around a screen and the skill of our fingers. As Aristotle said: "Man by nature is a social animal"; the attention market has made it possible for people who, for various reasons, previously did not socialize in real life, now do so digitally, even with large numbers of friends, that in reality would never be present. And this is a big problem because it leaves gaps that are filled by the unreal. All this causes the amounts of cortisol[13] generated by social networks to be extremely alarming. Dr. Marian Rojas points out the following:

---

12. Ibíd.

13. Cortisol is the stress hormone and is mainly secreted in moments of alert or threat. Its usefulness lies in the fact that it helps us to face challenges and threats with fight and flight mechanisms. In other words, this hormone is good for the body; what is harmful is the excess of it. For more information see Marian Rojas Estapé "Encuentra tu persona vitamina" (Find Your Vitamin Person) (Edit. Planeta. Mexico 2021) P. 26.

"The problem with cortisol is its constant release. Faced with a situation of great uncertainty or concern, the body becomes intoxicated with cortisol, that is, there are too many levels of this substance circulating in the blood. This picture of intoxication will modify the response of the immune and inflammatory system. A person who lives with high levels of cortisol due to a state of stress or alertness, maintaining over time, slows down the body's ability to regulate inflammation and the body has more difficulty defending itself against threats and, therefore, in these situations we are more vulnerable to infection."[14]

If we add to this comment all the pathologies mentioned above, it is not surprising why the population remains intoxicated by cortisol. I've known kids who live with high stress from video games, worried that they can't beat their opponent. Similarly, some celebrities get too stressed thinking about their social media posts, because if their fans don't respond as expected, they get depressed. I have friends who are aware of everything that happens in the lives of their ex-partners, others for sports, those who believe the "fake news", and so we could continue... for examples abound. Therefore, the state of stress generated by the digital world and social networks is extremely alarming.

This cyberspace is mutilating our sensitivity as we increasingly depend on our electronic devices. People prefer to be taking photos, recording videos or broadcasting their activities live, instead of enjoying them, even in the Christian community, when the center of the meeting is to worship God (Ephesians 4:17 & 19).

---

14. Ibíd. P. 28

We cannot stop the digital advance or everything that is behind it, but as Christians we can make a difference, bearing witness in the digital age and especially in the ideological phenomena that move in the technological revolution because only in this way will Christianity present a defense in this post-truth era, which we will be developing next.

Chapter 6

The Post-Truth Era

We are in times when the absolute truths are in a vacuum, where the superficial disconnects us from reality. In the post-truth era nothing is permanent, since everything is changing. Society is liquid and its composition lacks solidity. Now it all comes down to opinion; the post-truth era is the consolidation of relativism.

The year 2016 was classified by many journalists and political analysts as the year of "post-truth". This was the chosen word of the year by Oxford Dictionaries. Its meaning refers to something that denotes circumstances in which objective facts are less influential in shaping public opinion than appeals to personal emotions and beliefs.[1] The word "post-truth" was used for the first time in the American press in 1992 in an article by Steve Tesich for The Nation Magazine. Tesich, writing about the Watergate scandals and the Iraq war, indicated that at that time we had already accepted to live in a post-truth era, in which lies are indiscriminate and facts are hidden. However, it was in the book "The Post-Truth Era" (2004), by Ralph Keyes[2], when the

---

1. See https://www.oxfordlearnersdictionaries.com/us/definition/english/post-truth?q=post-truth.

2. Keyes indicated at the time that we live in the age of post-truth because

term found a certain conceptual development.[3] Christianity has always defended the truth and will continue to do so. However, all this dizzying system in communication causes a vacuum to be organized with respect to the truth of Christianity.

In a telephone conversation with Gonzalo Chamorro[4], we talked about the post-truth era and the weaknesses of the Church that must be strengthened in the face of the moral crisis that is growing disproportionately; and we conclude that it is urgent to reflect and work since we have been concerned with preaching more the message of salvation without the authenticity of a Christ who is the absolute foundation of Christianity.

To delve into this, we will divide this chapter into The Void of Truth and The Church Facing Ideologies.

1.   The Void of Truth

This new worldview of liquid modernity has managed to leave

---

his creed has taken hold among us: creative manipulation can take us beyond the realm of mere accuracy into a realm of truth-telling. The embellished information is presented as true in its spirit, and more true than the truth itself. For more information, the article published by the University of Navarra is recommended https:// www.unav.edu/web/ciencia-razón-y-fe/la-era-de-la-posverdad-la-posveracidad-y-la - quackery.

3. Ibíd.

4. Gonzalo A. Chamorro is Chilean, having his Bachelor's and Master's degrees from the Central American Theological Seminary (SETECA) in Guatemala City, Guatemala. He is currently writing his doctoral dissertation in colonial history. (PhD, from the Francisco Marroquín University) Founder of the Instituto CRUX. Professor of Theology and History, host of the radio program Café, Cultura y Cristianismo (Coffee, Culture, and Christianity). Lecturer, writer and researcher. Gonzalo has written for: Cuadernos de teología (Theology Notebooks), Theologicum, Líder Juvenil (Youth Leader), and Fe y Libertad (Faith and Freedom). In addition, he is the author of the book «Teología de la Unidad» (Theology of Unity) and co-author of other works.

the truth in a vacuum. Pluralism is itself an ideology because it declares that the claims of each religion are equally valid and therefore worthy of our respect.[5] In other words, pluralism proposes that we must affirm the independent value of each belief and religion and abandon the idea of converting people to the truth of Christ since all paths can save us. On this, Luis Seguí points out:

> *"He who promotes an absolute truth is one step away from becoming a criminal."*[6]

This affirmation defends the idea that the only thing that absolute truth achieves is to promote evil because it divides people into the fact that they believe it is the right one, and this only further fuels discrimination, causing hatred towards others to increase, as we see it in the practice of Muslim fundamentalism or the criminality that provoked the Inquisition.[7] For those who have embraced the idea of pluralism, nothing annoys them more than the idea of world evangelization. The modern world encourages pragmatism where we no longer question whether it is true; we are only interested in whether it will give us a result. That is to say, there is no longer a deep analysis of the ideas, we are only interested in knowing if we will have benefits without effort and without sacrifice. The problem with this is that the

---

5. John Stott "Llamados a ser diferentes" (People Called to be Different) (Edit. IIDENF, Costa Rica 1998) P. 43

6. Luis Seguí is a psychoanalyst, author of several works, see "Debate sobre el mal" (Debate On Evil), published April 17, 2014, https://youtu.be/xDWx-wytwGrQ (January 10, 2020).

7. One of the cruel events was that of the Inquisition that was carried out in the name of God, torture was the essential element for them to renounce their beliefs, otherwise they would die. See: Beatriz Comella, "La Inquisición española" (The Spanish Inquisition) (Edit. Rialp Madrid 2004), P 177.

absolute truths are left in the void and cannot be passed on to the next generation.

One of the characteristics that we see in the liquid society is that it no longer believes in absolutes due to its constant changes, that is why there is a rejection when we talk about the message of Jesus, mainly, due to the range of mystical knowledge of the supernatural because it concludes that no one he has the authority, simply, because he has disassociated himself from believing in an absolute truth and doubts everything. Everything that is differential is because it is distinct, however, the liquid man is not capable of recognizing if there is an absolute truth capable of changing human life, since believing in it only leads him to the path of fanaticism. However, God has made us thinking beings, for this very reason He considers us responsible for the knowledge we have. The Apostle Paul writes:

"For this reason we also, since the day we heard it, do not cease to pray for you, and to ask that you may be filled with the knowledge of His will in all wisdom and spiritual understanding; that you may walk worthy of the Lord, fully pleasing Him, being fruitful in every good work and increasing in the knowledge of God"
(Colossians 1:9-10)

Paul encourages us to grow in the knowledge that will arouse that intellectual curiosity by wanting to know more and grow in the wisdom of God in the face of the threats of this world. Although we must also recognize that when we reject an absolute truth, we do so knowingly because that is the only way to justify ourselves for our bad deeds, so as not to feel guilty. The letter to the Romans tells us about it:

As it is written: "There is none righteous, no, not one; There is none who understands; There is none who seeks after God. They have all turned aside; They have together become unprofitable; There is none who does good, no, not one." "Their throat is an open tomb; With their tongues they have practiced deceit" "The poison of asps is under their lips"; "Whose mouth is full of cursing and bitterness." "Their feet are swift to shed blood; Destruction and misery are in their ways; And the way of peace they have not known." "There is no fear of God before their eyes."
(Romans 3:10-18)

This verse tells us that when we have not lived by Christian standards we easily deviate from the path because there is no foundation that defines us and a light to follow. So, how can we recognize what is the truth and how to stay in it?

In the Gospel of John, the writer emphasizes announcing that Jesus is the Only Truth. If we analyze this chapter we find the following:

- Jesus testifies of the truth before Pilate (John 18:37).
- If it is not through HIM, there is no way to the truth (John 14:6).
- He was full of truth (John 1:14).
- There is no truth in the devil (John 8:44).

Paul develops Christian theology by telling us what to do with the truth:

- We must love truth so as not to perish (2 Thessalonians 2:10). We must believe it (2 Thessalonians 2:12,13).
- We must seek approval (2 Timothy 2:15).

- We must manifest it (2 Corinthians 4:2).
- We must obey it (Galatians 3:1).
- We must acknowledge it (2 Timothy 2:25).

These are some examples, however, we can conclude that there is no one who can really fill our lives like Jesus does. Because only He is: The Way, The Truth and The Life.[8]

For all of the above, this section concludes by quoting John Stott in the face of the range of existing controversies in the vacuum of truth: *"Against the challenge of pluralism we must be a community that declares the truth and defends the unique character of Jesus Christ."*[9] If we live in the authenticity of Christ, we will be able to have clarity with arguments to present a defense in the era of "post-truth" where ideologies flood us. We will talk about this next.

2.   The Church Facing Ideologies

At present we see the great influence that all currents of thought have and that sadly ends up affecting Christianity. The statistics reflect the ups and downs in the active members of the congregations, data that increased after the coronavirus pandemic in 2020.

The diversity of factors that influence this are too many, for example: divisions for doctrinal, personal or institutional reasons. Those who stray from the ways of God. Those who point to Christianity as hypocritical. The intellectuals who deny

---

8. John 14:6

9. John Stott, "El discípulo radical" (The Radical Disciple) op. cit. P. 24.

it and embrace the aphorism of Friedrich Nietzsche ("God is dead. God remains dead. We have killed him."[10]), the rise of atheism, nihilism and all ideologies. More than a century has passed, but I believe that the conclusion that Nietzsche focused on still stands as the factors determining this result. First, the cowardice of the Church for not defending its values, and second, hypocrisy.[11]

In the committee for world evangelization, popularly known as the Lausanne Movement[12], organized by Billy Graham and John Stott, celebrated in the 20th century, it is necessary to remember what the latter said:

"The Church is growing like never before, but without depth."

This affirmation is more than revealing because it continues to be the great problem in our days because a little-demanding God is preached, made in the image of postmodern man who is content with an abstract and idealistic love far from the fraternal or social commitment[13] in which experiences are the only criterion of truth.

For this reason it is important to reflect and not respond with hatred demonizing the side that we believe is not the right one, because we cannot fall into the enemy's trap. As we well

---

10. Friedrich Nietzsche, "Así habló Zaratustra" (Thus spoke Zarathustra) (E-books 2010), P. 15.

11. For more information, see the article by Dr. Gonzalo Chamorro at www.intitutocrux.org/blogs/buen-arbol/etica/2019/09/la-transmutacion-de-to-dos-los-valores/.

12. For more information see:: www.lausanne.org/johnstott.

13. Antonio Cruz, "Postmodernidad" (Postmodernity) op. cit. P. 170.

know, the fight is spiritual, not against people; let us see the importance of obedience and testimony because they are the way to counteract all this disobedience that contradicts what is established by God, as indicated by the Scripture:

"For though we walk in the flesh, we do not war according to the flesh. For the weapons of our warfare are not carnal but mighty in God for pulling down strongholds, casting down arguments and every high thing that exalts itself against the knowledge of God, bringing every thought into captivity to the obedience of Christ, and being ready to punish all disobedience when your obedience is fulfilled." (2 Corinthians 10:3-6)

Fortresses are built by the mental structures of the diversity of currents that we see in this liquid society. Faced with this, we must eradicate what is not right before God and return to the Sacred Text, meekly correcting as children of God in unity, in love and in the defense of our faith, all those who demand a reason for the hope that there is in us.[14]

This is the DNA of the matter: What is the reason for the little defense against ideologies? The answer is simply because there is no debate on ideas due to the lack of meekness that occurs due to the following factors: the lack of knowledge due to lack of training, and there is no training due to little interest in reading and research, and now not to mention delving into the Holy Scriptures. The contemporary world, as Stott mentions, has given birth to the twins "lack of reflection and sense"[15], because

---

14. 1 Peter 3:15

15. For further study see John Stott, "Cómo desarrollar una mente cristiana" (How to Develop a Christian Mind), http:/www.iglesiareformada/stott_desarrollar_mente.html

it is not interested in getting so complicated. In response to these twins, the Bible is forceful: *"Brethren, do not be children in understanding; however, in malice be babes, but in understanding be mature. (1 Corinthians 14:20)"*. Paul makes a distinction between the two spheres. On the one hand, he forbids them to be children and on the other hand he orders them to be. As for evil, one must be as innocent as a child, but in the area of thought one must grow and mature.[16] Sadly, this great dilemma is caused by the lack of character in the Church, for the simple reason, as we have emphasized, that "we want experience to be the only criterion of truth."[17]

As leaders we have the responsibility to pay more attention to the message we are taking to the world, because if there is no coherence between what we preach and what we live, we will only be proclaiming fanaticism. John Stott notes:[18]

"Many have zeal without knowledge, enthusiasm without instruction. Enthusiasm is good. But God wants both: enthusiasm directed by knowledge, and knowledge inflamed by enthusiasm. As John Mackay expressed it: 'Commitment without reflection is fanaticism in action; but reflection without commitment is the paralysis of all action.'"

This is controversial since, in recent decades, as a Church we have been guided more by experience than by knowledge,

---

16. Ibíd.

17. Cited by the unpublished material of Instituto Crux, for more information see Instituto Crux Ideology "La mente Cristiana" (The Christian Mind) can be consulted on the website: www.institutocrux.org.

18. John Stott, "Creer es también pensar" (Your Mind Matters) (Edit. Certeza, Buenos Aires 1996). P.9.

and it is not that experience is wrong, but the correct thing is the balance of both: experience plus knowledge. Because on the one hand we have those who are only 'experience' and become mystics who end up making heresies, and on the other hand those who are only 'knowledge', but unfortunately do not produce anything. Meanwhile, the new generations are no longer interested in history and delving into the Holy Scriptures, since they are guided by an unbiblical emotionalism. Their main argument is that God humiliates the intellectual because he becomes self-centered, and it is true, God humiliates the one who exalts himself, but He never despises the mind that He himself has created.[19] Stott adds:

"Believing is also thinking, faith and reason are not opposed, the specter of anti-intellectualism rises regularly to threaten the Christian church."[20]

We live in a society in which, mainly, manipulation rides for the emancipation of the "hybrid theology" that circulates in our midst, in which some ideologies are supported. It is our responsibility at this crossroads to search the Scriptures, to ensure that our faith is truly a faith grounded in the Gospel.[21] Because in this way, what we have to change will be revealed, as the writer of Hebrews mentions:

---

19. Ibíd. P. 10

20. Ibíd.

21. "Christian theology is at a crossroads. We are faced with the inescapable duty of searching the Scriptures for…We have to listen and evaluate new ideas, with a humble and deeply critical mind. Taken from the unpublished material of the Crux Institute, which quotes Juan Stam in this commentary. Instituto Crux, Ideology "La mente Cristiana" (The Christian Mind) (2018), P.22 See: www.institutocrux.org.

"For the word of God is living and powerful, and sharper than any two-edged sword, piercing even to the division of soul and spirit, and of joints and marrow, and is a discerner of the thoughts and intents of the heart." (Hebrews 4:12)

Taking into account this verse and everything exposed in this section, Christianity must be aware of and responsible for this reality. Christianity must respond with that authenticity that shows that in the face of all these ideologies we are the resistance, because in Scripture we find the only way to renew our way of thinking and make the radical change in the human being, that leads us to the fullness of life that is Jesus.

We'll move on to our last chapter to expand on what we need to do in the face of this cultural battle to uphold the truth.

Chapter 7

Practical Advice In The Cultural Battle

In Luke 4:46-49 we find a very revealing passage for these times because it not only illustrates the way in which we should base our lives but also the importance of obeying His commandments. *"To confess that Jesus Christ is our Lord, but not to obey Him is to build our lives on sand."*[1] If we build our lives on the sand, we will be easily carried away by the currents that run in times where liquid modernity rampages without mercy, tearing down Christian morality, but if we build our lives on the Rock that is Christ, we will be unshakable and, therefore, we will have arguments. and credibility to present a defense of our faith in this cultural battle that is taking place.

We have considered dividing this chapter into: Called To Be Different and We Cannot Adapt.

1.   Called To Be Different

Christianity must respond to this call because we are the remnant to testify in the midst of this moral crisis in which we live within the cultural battle and that unbalances the behavior of the individual. It is enough to see some faces of the citizens

---

1.   John Stott, "El discípulo radical" (The Radical Disciple), op. cit. P.22.

that reflect despair and concern. The great diseases of the 21st century are "depression" and "anxiety" and when they do not know how to manage them, they can lead to suicide; both are nothing more than the result of the lack of meaning to live. Viktor Frankl determines this human condition as the existential void[2] that is nothing more than the lack of meaning of life in the human being.

We live in a society that cries out for help due to the lack of meaning in life. Jesus said: "...*for without Me you can do nothing*."[3] The existential void reflects to us the absence of Christ in people's lives. This was precisely what happened in the encounter that Jesus had with the Samaritan woman[4] in John 4:13-14. If the human being essentially perishes, it is because his source of meaning is not Christ.

The gospel message is still standing and has not changed or been modified, and despite so many social changes we must continue to proclaim that Jesus is the source of meaning and that the springs of life flow through Him. Jesus did it in the midst of a party:

---

2. The existential emptiness manifests itself above all in a state of boredom. The loss of the feeling that life is meaningful. See Viktor Frankl "El hombre en busca de sentido" (Man's Search for Meaning), (Edit. Herder, Barcelona.1991) P. 60.

3. John 15:5

4. Jesus implied that the human psyche is an energy field that has a continuous and inevitable flow of thoughts and emotions and that this flow constitutes the greatest source of human entertainment. But he wanted to transform that source, enrich it, make it stable and lasting. In the dialogue with the Samaritan woman, he addressed the enrichment of that vital flow in contrast to the existential dissatisfaction produced by the human failure to try to conquer a continuous account of pleasure. For more information on the analysis of the intelligence of Christ, it is recommended, Augusto Cury "El maestro de maestros" (The Teacher of Teachers) (Edit. Grupo Nelson Nashville 2008) P. 70

"On the last day, that great day of the feast, Jesus stood and cried out, saying, "If anyone thirsts, let him come to Me and drink. He who believes in Me, as the Scripture has said, out of his heart will flow rivers of living water." (John 7:37-38)

At that time Jesus did not speak of rules of behavior, criticism of immorality or religious knowledge. He preached about the need to live with pleasure in its broadest sense. He affirmed that He could produce full satisfaction, an emotional ecstasy capable of solving people's existential anguish.[5]

Christ revolutionized the character of the human being. He was different, His thought broke the prevailing social parameters of His time. The people who followed Him began to see life completely differently and that caused them to love or reject Him. The legacy of Christianity has continued for more than 2 thousand years; we are its representatives on Earth, so we have to make turbulence through the thought of Christ.

We must never forget that Christianity is a counterculture and has survived through history. The Roman Empire tried to kill it, but every time they killed ten, another hundred would rise up and say *"kill us too"*. If we live as Christians they will not be able to destroy us.

Let's reflect on the following: the Church that dies is because it began to rot from the inside. The tree that is uprooted by the storm is because its heart is rotten, otherwise the storm would not be able to bring it down. Therefore, if the Church falls due to all these ideological currents, it is because it was dead before it fell.

---

5. Ibíd. P.69

We must recognize that we need to rebuild the Christian faith and go back to Scripture. It is important that we be realistic, because we are a Church that has been called out of the world to belong to Him and sent back to the world for service and witness. The apostle Paul is very clear to be different: (Ephesians 4:17-19, 21-24). The call is significant, we must be different from the culture that surrounds us. This can only happen with the character of Christ because it is what gives us the ability to face all kinds of circumstances[6] and, furthermore, it strongly marks that distinction in society. Dallas Willard expands: "*Jesus Christ not only came to give us the gift of eternal life through the atonement but also He came to revolutionize the character of human conduct.*"[7] The message of Jesus has become universal and also enhances the character of everyone who decides to follow Him; He calls us to be different in order to make a difference in this world (1 Thessalonians 1:8-10).

In our last section we will see that an authentic life in Jesus will not allow us to adapt to the system of this world.

2.   We Cannot Adapt

The Church must always follow the path of the gospel, without altering it or changing what is already established in the Scriptures. Times change, forms change, systems change, but God's Word remains forever.

In every era of history (scientific, industrial, communications, philosophical, sexual and social) there have been revolutionary

---

6.   Philippians 4:13

7.   Dallas Willard, "Renueva tu corazón, sé cómo Cristo" (Renovation of the Heart: Putting on the Character of Christ) (Edit. Clie. Barcelona 2004).

changes. We cannot deny that change produces progress, but as long as it does not affect or put our values at risk and, above all, the faith we profess. The apostle John is blunt on this subject:

"Do not love the world or the things in the world. If anyone loves the world, the love of the Father is not in him. For all that is in the world—the lust of the flesh, the lust of the eyes, and the pride of life—is not of the Father but is of the world. And the world is passing away, and the lust of it; but he who does the will of God abides forever." (1 John 2:15-17)

In other words, we belong to this world, but we cannot adapt to what goes against Scripture. We are called to be the hallmark in society. Jesus was a radical for His time, He never intended to adapt to the world; as His message spread, people adapted to Him. We must continue with that legacy because we cannot be one of the people who, for fear of persecution and social shame, end up approving of the world's system and its ideologies, because if we adapt, we are dead in life. I emphasize, if we adapt we are lost, but if we dare to be different and resist to defend the truth, the *world* will have to adapt. Probably not all will, but there will be a group that will. Some will hate us, others will love us, but the important thing is that, through the resistance to defend the truth, the world can see the message of Christ reflected in our lives.

With this I do not pretend that we emancipate hatred towards those who think differently. Let us remember that all the totalitarian movements that have arisen in revolutions have led us to violence in order to impose their ideologies, however, when we talk about not adapting, we mean being revolutionaries of the character of the human being, just as Jesus did without the use of violence, but love.

Jesus hung out with sinners, prostitutes, pagans, corrupt politicians, and even broke religious stereotypes in order to reach these people, but just because He was around them, and even ate with them, didn't mean He adapted to their lifestyle; the effect of the message of Jesus through His testimony made people adapt to Him.

In short, we have a great responsibility. Some might question it, saying 'it's a very big world', 'I can't handle everyone', it's not necessary; it is enough to start from our house with the family. We cannot continue ignoring the reality in which we live, on the contrary, we must be *"doers of the word, and not hearers only"* (James 1:22-27).

Being doers of His word will keep us firm so as not to adapt to the world system, which will mean that there has been a genuine renewal in our lives and for that we must remember four important things that the Church of the first century practiced (Acts 2:42- 47). First: it was a Church that remained in the doctrine, that is, in the principles of Christianity. Second: It was a Church that cared. Third: a Church that adored, and fourth: it was one that evangelized through its testimony because they found grace and favor before the people.

In this same way we must act, preaching through our testimony so that in the society we live in, we find grace and favor, and in this way, God continues adding to all who must be saved.

So far we have developed this fascinating subject with the intention of achieving greater resistance through the values that only Christianity can give us in the face of the great dilemmas of the 21st century.

The challenge is huge, but I assure you that it will be worth it.

Conclusions

We have reached the end of this journey. Throughout the study of this book, we observed the importance of Christianity in society. It is up to us to make the conclusions corresponding to each chapter, hoping with this to continue contributing to the academy and, especially, to each person interested in the subject.

Chapter 1

- Ideologies are statist because they seek public policies to become legal and thus impose themselves. While ideas are dynamic and are developed by brilliant minds in search of the truth.

- God has given us the ability to think, reason and create. The words knowledge, wisdom and intelligence are constantly mentioned by the apostle Paul, let us note that he considered them essential for the Christian life.

Chapter 2

- Faced with the threat that is given by the manipulation of language, we must eradicate by example to demonstrate that values can be sustained through a Christian faith, despite the constant and aggressive bombardment.

- Inclusive language tries to modify words, but that will not eliminate discrimination, since that corresponds to the evil that occurs in the heart. The best way to deal with this is by being better people every day, through faith in Christ, in a community of love for others.

Chapter 3

- Faced with the constant threat of totalitarian ideologies and categories in social changes, we must adhere to the Holy Scriptures to remain with dignity in the image of God, of whom we were created.

- The drastic reduction of the world population through abortion and euthanasia is the successful advancement of gender ideology, regardless of the fact that all this cost is the death of innocents. Christianity must be very responsible and respond in favor of life, since the decision of when to end life belongs to God.

Chapter 4

- Marriage is not a human invention. God established it from creation as a partnership covenant between man and woman, therefore, it is important to have a proper perspective of marriage for the correct structure of the family.

- Family is essential for the education of children and for the benefit of society as a whole. Let us remember that culture is sown from the family, so if it is destroyed, culture disintegrates. Behind the new family configurations is the devilish plan. Christianity must defend the nuclear family, training the new generations in Judeo-Christian principles.

Chapter 5

- The digital world has benefited us, however, every day it immerses us more in a current in which we are controlled and trapped by the system that makes us dependent on the digital age.

- The world of entertainment helps us to have pleasant moments of fun, and social networks are good with the correct use, however, they should not become an addiction that generates pathologies and they should never replace our values.

Chapter 6

- The post-truth era is based on the opinion of others, pluralism and relativism are taking us down a current in which absolute truths are being left in a vacuum, so Christianity must be a community of obedience that defends the truth and uniqueness of Christ.

- It is our responsibility at this crossroads to search the Scriptures, to ensure that our faith is truly a faith grounded in the Gospel. (1 Corinthians 3:11)

Chapter 7

- When we talk about being outliers to the world, it makes a counterculture, which means that Christianity has values contrary to today's society. Jesus was an outlier in his time and established the moral standards that revolutionized human behavior.

- The Christian Church has remained firm in its principles and values throughout the centuries and has shown that being different has made changes in the history of humanity. Despite the fact that the Church has been threatened, God has always raised up a remnant to remain fastened to the Holy Scriptures.

The objective of this contribution is to expand knowledge to train and equip ourselves to face the challenges of the contemporary world, because all these dilemmas can only be eradicated with the Word of God and His presence. As it is written:

"All Scripture is given by inspiration of God, and is profitable for doctrine, for reproof, for correction, for instruction in righteousness, that the man of God may be complete, thoroughly equipped for every good work." (2 Timothy 3:16-17)

Bibliography

Dictionaries and Bibles

1. Diccionario Enciclopédico Bíblico Ilustrado (Illustrated Biblical Encyclopedic Dictionary), Edit. Clie. Barcelona 2016
2. New King James Version, https://www.biblegateway.com

Theology Books

1. Raúl Zaldívar, Apocalípticism (Apocalypticism), Edit. Clie. Barcelona. 2012.
2. Raúl Zaldívar, Doctrina de Santidad (Holiness Doctrine), Edit. Clie. Barcelona. 2001.
3. John Stott, El discípulo radical (The Radical Disciple), Edit. Certeza, Argentina 2010.
4. Dallas Willard, Renueva tu corazón, sé cómo Cristo (Renovation of the Heart: Putting on the Character of Christ) Edit. Clie. Barcelona 2004.
5. John Stott, Creer es también pensar (Your Mind Matters), Edit. Certeza, Buenos Aires 1996.
6. John Stott, Llamados a ser diferentes (People Called to be Different), Edit. IIDENF, Costa Rica 1998.

History Books

1. Terry Eagleton Ideología (Ideology), Edit. Paidos, Buenos Aires 1997.
2. Beatriz Comella, La Inquisición española (The Spanish Inquisition), Edit. Rialp Madrid 2004.

Sociology Books

1. Zygmunt Bauman, Modernidad y Holocausto (Modernity and the Holocaust) Edit. Sequitur Madrid. 2006
2. Antonio Cruz, Postmodernidad (Postmodernity) Edit. Clie. Barcelona 2003.
3. Zygmunt Bauman, Modernidad Líquida (Liquid Modernity) Edit. FCE Argentina 2002.
4. Cesar Vidal, Un mundo que cambia (A World That Changes), Edit. Agustin Agency, Nashville 2020.
5. Agustín Laje, La batalla cultural (The Cultural Battle), Edit. Harper Collins México 2022.

Specialized Books

1. Juan Varela, Homosexualidad (Homosexuality) Barcelona: Editorial Clie, 2016.
2. Catherine Scheraldi and Miguel Núñez, Revolución sexual (Sexual Revolution) Edit. B&H TN. 2018.
3. Bernal, A. O. F. de psicología jurídica e investigación C. (Fundamentals of Legal Psychology and Criminal Investigation), Edit. Salamanca 2009.
4. Juan Varela and M. Mar Molina, Tu matrimonio si importa (Your Marriage Does Matter), Edit. Clie Barcelona 2012.
5. Bruno Patino, La civilización de la memoria de pez (The Fish Memory Civilization), Edit. Alinza, Madrid 2020.

6. Marian Rojas Estapé, Encuentra tu persona vitamina (Find Your Vitamin Person), Edit. Planeta. México 2021.

Other Sources

1. Nicolás M. and Agustín L. El libro negro de la nueva izquierda (The Black Book of the New Left), Edit. Grupo Unión.
2. Jim Newheiser, Matrimonio, Divorcio y Nuevo M. (Marriage, Divorce and Remarriage) Edit. Poiema Col. 2019.
3. Ayn Rand, The Virtue of Selfishness, Edit. Signet USA 1964.
4. Guadalupe Batallán, Dignos hasta el final (Worthy to the End), E-books.
5. Eduardo Galeano, Las venas abiertas de América latina (The Open Veins of Latin America), Edit. S. XXI México 2004.
6. Arts. 209-214, Rep. 5.9 Pol. 7.14.10, Apología contra gentiles (Apology Against Gentiles), XI 8.
7. Viktor Frankl, El hombre en busca de sentido (Man's Search for Meaning), Edit. Herder, Barcelona. 1991.
8. Paul Enns, Compendio portavoz de teología (The Moody Handbook of Theology), Edit Chicago, 2008.
9. Friedrich Nietzsche "Así habló Zaratustra" (Thus Spoke Zarathustra) (E-books 2010).
10. Augusto Cury, El maestro de maestros (The Teacher of Teachers), Edit. Grupo Nelson Nashville 2008.

Websites

1. www.plannedparenthood.org
2. César Vidal, "La manipulación del lenguaje" (The Manipulation of Language) conference published June 7 2019

https://youtu.be/FqjVc6BRuKU (January 7 2020).

3. Santiago Bilinkis, "Como nos manipula las redes sociales" (How Social Networks Manipulate Us), published November 27 2019; https://youtu.be/8nKCA9h-7BA (February 7 2020).

4. Agustín Laje "Ideología de Género y Aborto conferencia" (Gender Ideology and Abortion Conference) published November 16 2021 See. https://youtu.be/EU4G5RsE0vs (November 18 2022).

5. Agustín Laje, La ideología de género aplasta la libertad (Gender Ideology Crushes Freedom). published March 5 2019. https://youtu.be/RDeoYGq2GHM (November 19 2022).

6. Luis Seguí "Debate sobre el mal" (Debate On Evil) April 17 2014, https://youtu.be/xDWxwytwGrQ (January 10 2020)

7. Gonzalo Chamorro www.intitutocrux.org/blogs/buen-arbol/etica/2019/09/ la-transmutación-de-todos-los-valores/

8. www.lausanne.org/johnstott

9. www.dle.rae.es

10. John Stott, "Cómo desarrollar una mente cristiana" (How to Develop a Christian Mind), http:/www.iglesia-reformada/stott_desarrollar_mente.html

11. www.institutocrux.org

12. www.memoria.fahce.unlp.edu.ar

13. www.un.org (viewed 11-18-2022).

14. www.revistadelauniversidad.mx (11-19-2022).

15. Universidad Autónoma de México https://ciencia.unam.mx/leer/963/-sabes-que-es-la-intersexualidad-

16. www.plannedparenthood.org/es/temas-de-salud/aborto/todavia-es-legal-obtener-un aborto?

17. https://www.lavanguardia.com/mu-
yfan/20190606/462706545782/miley-cyrus-aborto-
desnudo-instagram.html
18. https://www.ucc.edu.ar/mediosucc/ve_detras_del_abor-
to_presion_internacional_agustin_laje_escritor_dio_
una_conferencia_en_la_arena_sonora-8056.html/
19. https://www.un.org/sustainabledevelopment/es/poverty/
20. https://observatoriofiex.es/diversidad-familiar-los-
diferentes-tipos-de-familia/
21. www.lanacion.com.ar
22. https://www.oxfordlearnersdictionaries.com/us/defini-
tion/english/post-truth?q=post-truth.
23. https://www.unav.edu/web/ciencia-razon-y-fe/la-era-de-
la-posverdad-la-posveracidad-y-la-charlatanería.

Additional Author's Publications

Volviendo a la Esencia (Returning To The Essence), is an invitation from God to return to His embrace. The author challenges us in a very practical way to leave self-sufficiency, religious conformism and challenges us to turn to God.

Lo que hace la Fe (What Faith Does), this book does not seek to give simple formulas to achieve success or make spurious statements of faith, rather, its author tries to give an explanation based on the biblical text that leads us to show a faith that influences our practical life.

El Cristianismo ante la crisis moral del siglo XXI (Christianity in the Face of the Moral Crisis of the 21st Century). In this research you will be able to find anexcellent analysis of the different intricacies that have made Judeo-Christian values lose all relevance and influence in contemporary culture.

"Jesucristo: El camino, la verdad y la vida"
("Jesus Christ: The Way, the Truth and the Life")

www.ingramcontent.com/pod-product-compliance
Lightning Source LLC
Chambersburg PA
CBHW021844130726
47989CB00009B/3083